Other NEW YORKER Cartoon Books

THE
NEW YORKER
BOOK OF DOCTOR CARTOONS

THE
NEW YORKER
BOOK OF DOCTOR* CARTOONS
*AND PSYCHIATRIST

ALFRED A. KNOPF   NEW YORK 1994

THIS IS A BORZOI BOOK
PUBLISHED BY ALFRED A. KNOPF, INC.

ISBN 0-679-43069-5
LC 93-61390

Manufactured in the United States of America
Published December 1, 1993
Reprinted Four Times
Sixth Printing, August 1994

THE NEW YORKER

BOOK OF DOCTOR CARTOONS

"Well, what seems to be the trouble, Mr. Sims?"

"*Don't worry. Fantasies about devouring the doctor are perfectly normal.*"

"The doctor will see you now, Mrs. Perkins.
Please try not to upset him."

"Doctor, *you <u>must</u> stop addressing your Medicare patients as Comrade.*"

"I told him to lay off the high-fibre diet."

"Humph! You'd think it was the first appendectomy they ever saw."

"*I'm putting you on two earrings.*"

"Now just sit down and tell me what seems to be the trouble."

"It is unfortunate that I didn't get your case earlier, Mrs. Perkins."

"I had a touch of the flu last February, and that funny ache
in my thumb still flares up when it's damp, but, thanks to the
diet and exercise program you recommended, I feel better all
around since the last abduction."

"Have you spoken to an herbalist?"

"Dr. MacGruder says I must build myself up before I start reducing."

"Now inhale deeply, Mrs. Saunders."

"The doctor's lawyer will see you now."

"You said a moment ago that everybody you look at seems to be a rabbit.
Now just what do you mean by that, Mrs. Sprague?"

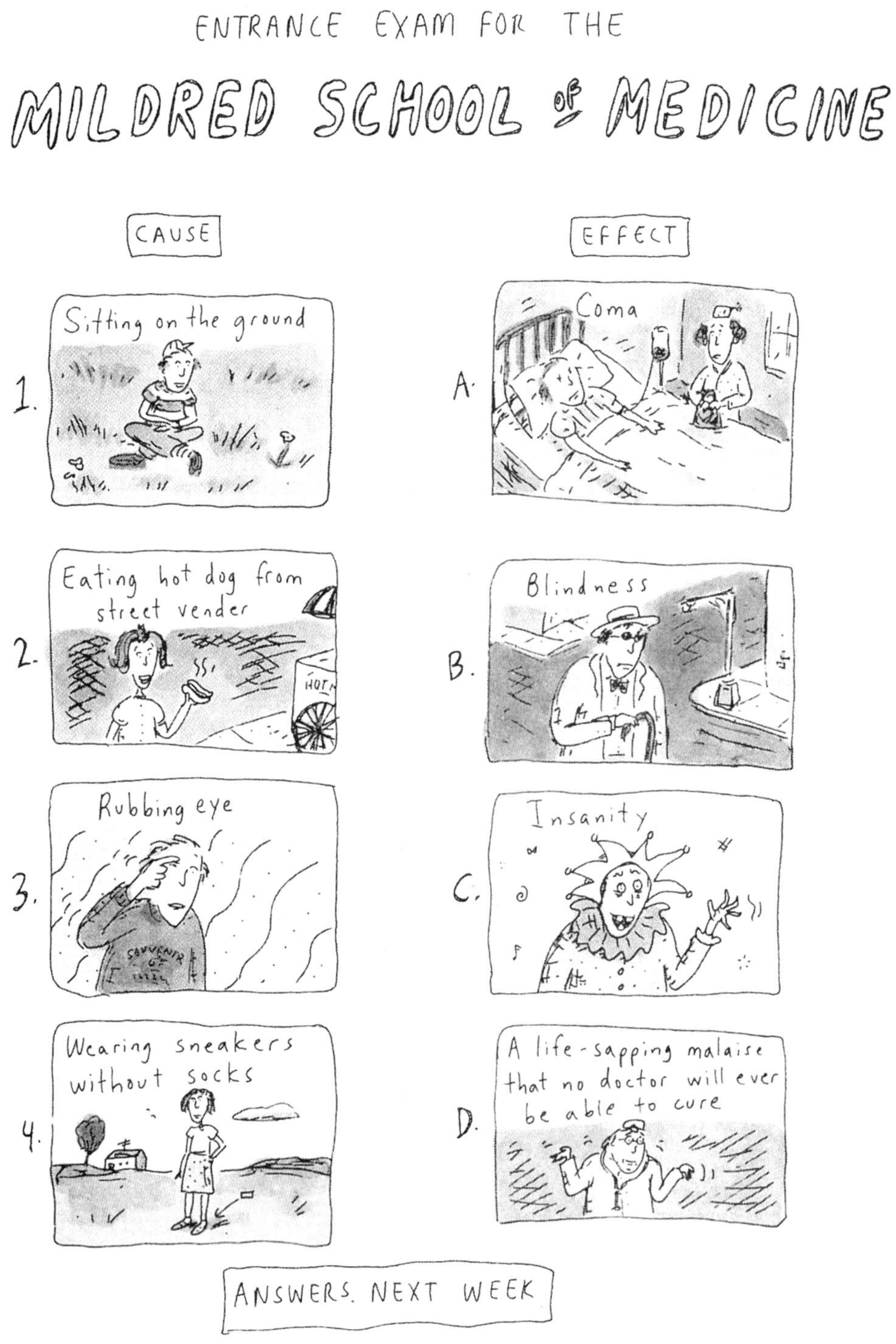
ENTRANCE EXAM FOR THE
MILDRED SCHOOL OF MEDICINE
CAUSE
EFFECT
1.
Sitting on the ground
2.
Eating hot dog from street vender
3.
Rubbing eye
4.
Wearing sneakers without socks
A.
Coma
B.
Blindness
C.
Insanity
D.
A life-sapping malaise that no doctor will ever be able to cure
ANSWERS NEXT WEEK
R. Chast

"I thought I'd give Western medicine one more chance."

"It's pronounced 'hee-la' monster. The 'g' sounds like an 'h.'"

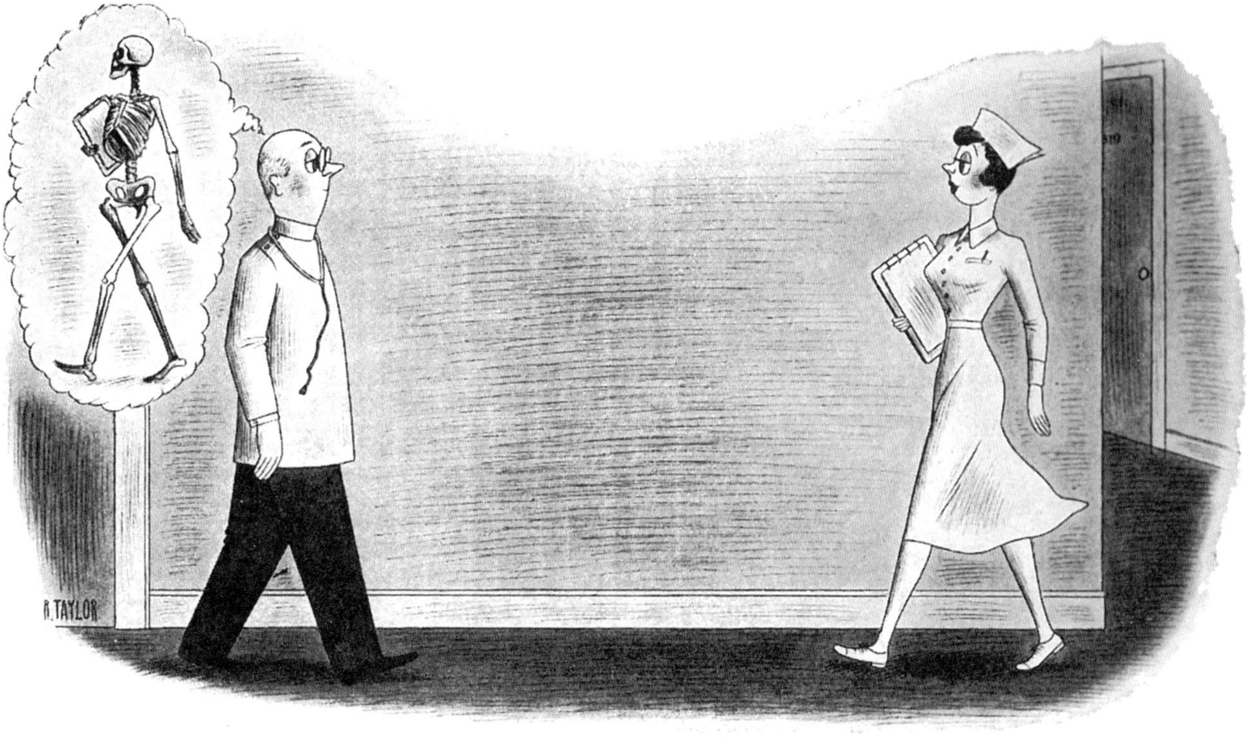
R. TAYLOR

"Want to hear something funny?"

"Does the doctor hug?"

"It's got to come out, of course, but that doesn't address the deeper problem."

"Yours is a vanishing breed, Doctor."

"The doctor will bill you now."

"'Is there a doctor in the house?' That's the call Harold's been waiting for since he started practice, twenty-five years ago."

*"What he needs is a change of scene. Why don't you
move him to some other window?"*

"... and now in this next scene you've graduated from medical school and
become the most famous neuropathologist in the world."

*"The Doctor isn't available right now. Would you like
to speak to Mr. Hyde?"*

"It's remarkable, Mr. Volmer. You have the
clothes of a man half your age!"

*"It means that in that complex machine of yours
a tonsil has gone haywire."*

"Well, Phil, after years of vague complaints and imaginary ailments, we finally have something to work with."

"*My advice to you, Mr. Weston, is that you relax your vigilance against Communism just a wee bit.*"

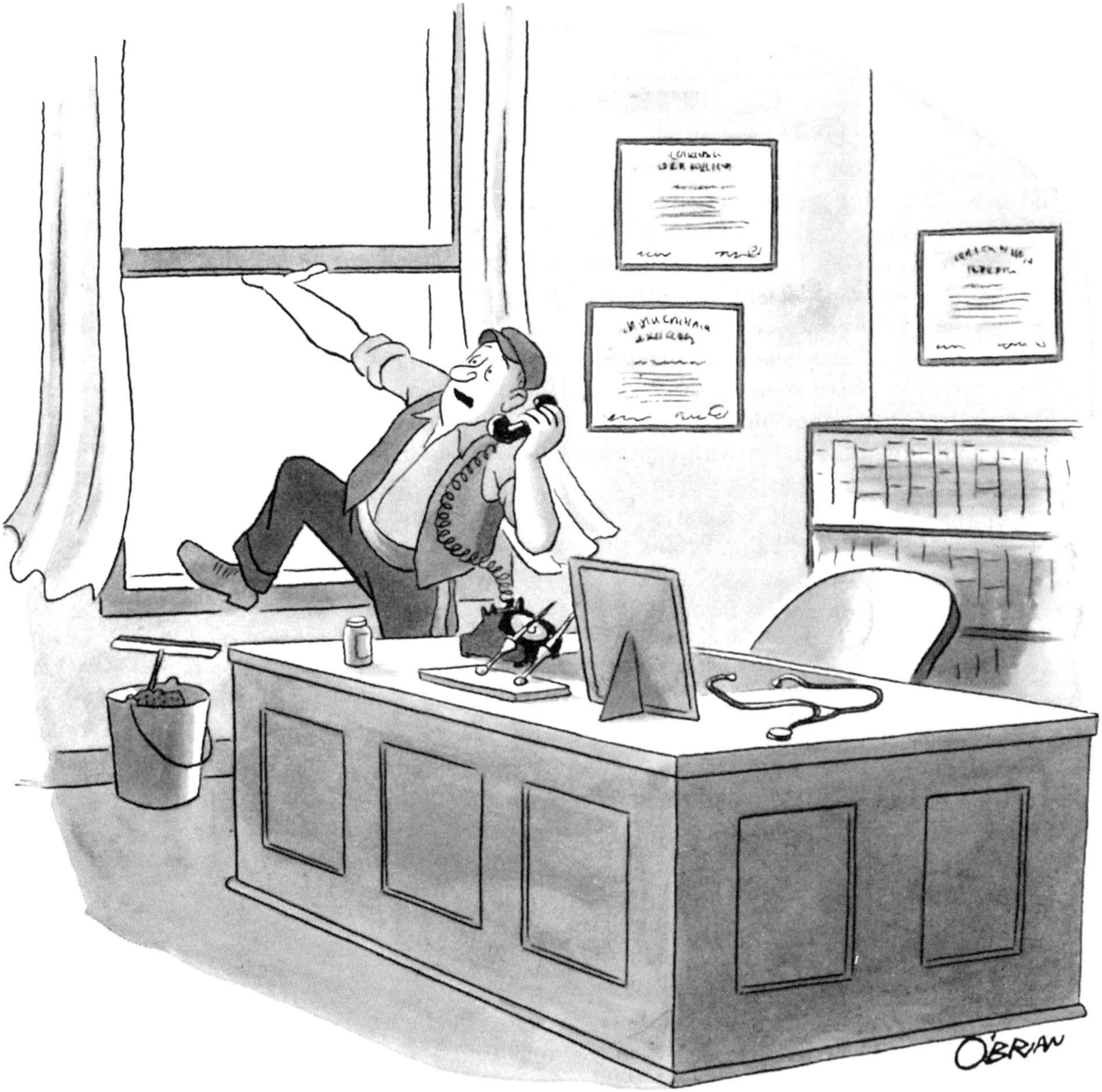
O'BRIAN

"Yes, I see. Well, there's a lot of it going around. Take a couple of aspirins, get a good night's sleep, and call again in the morning."

"Just give him lots and lots of love."

"You needn't feel guilty. You earned the fortune you inherited by giving her great happiness while she was alive."

"Good heavens, man, your heart is breaking!"

"Well, this is a very impressive résumé, young man. I think
you're going to make a fine patient."

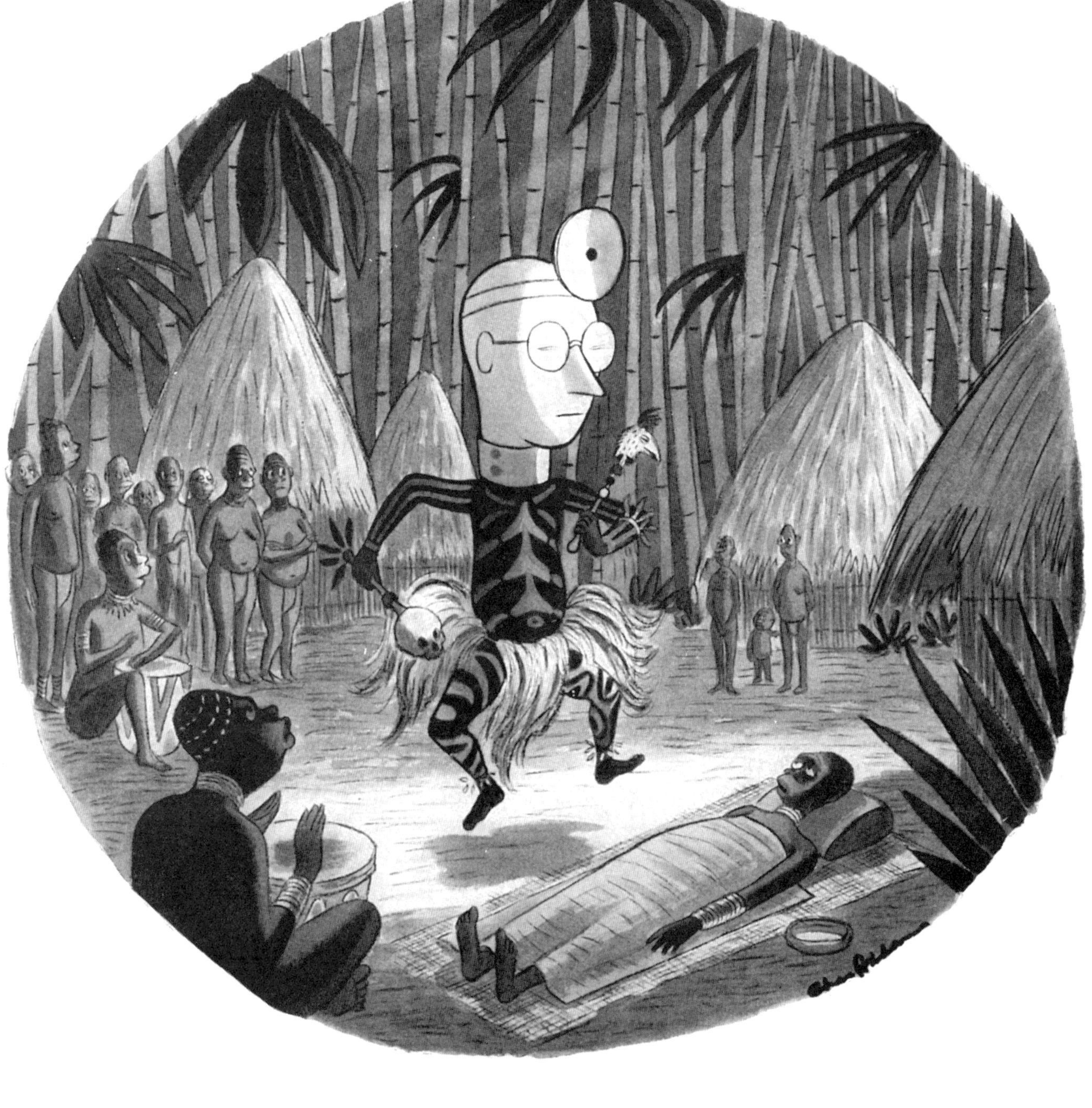

"The doctor is in court on Tuesdays and Wednesdays."

"*Naomi's shrink is a living national treasure. Isn't he, hon?*"

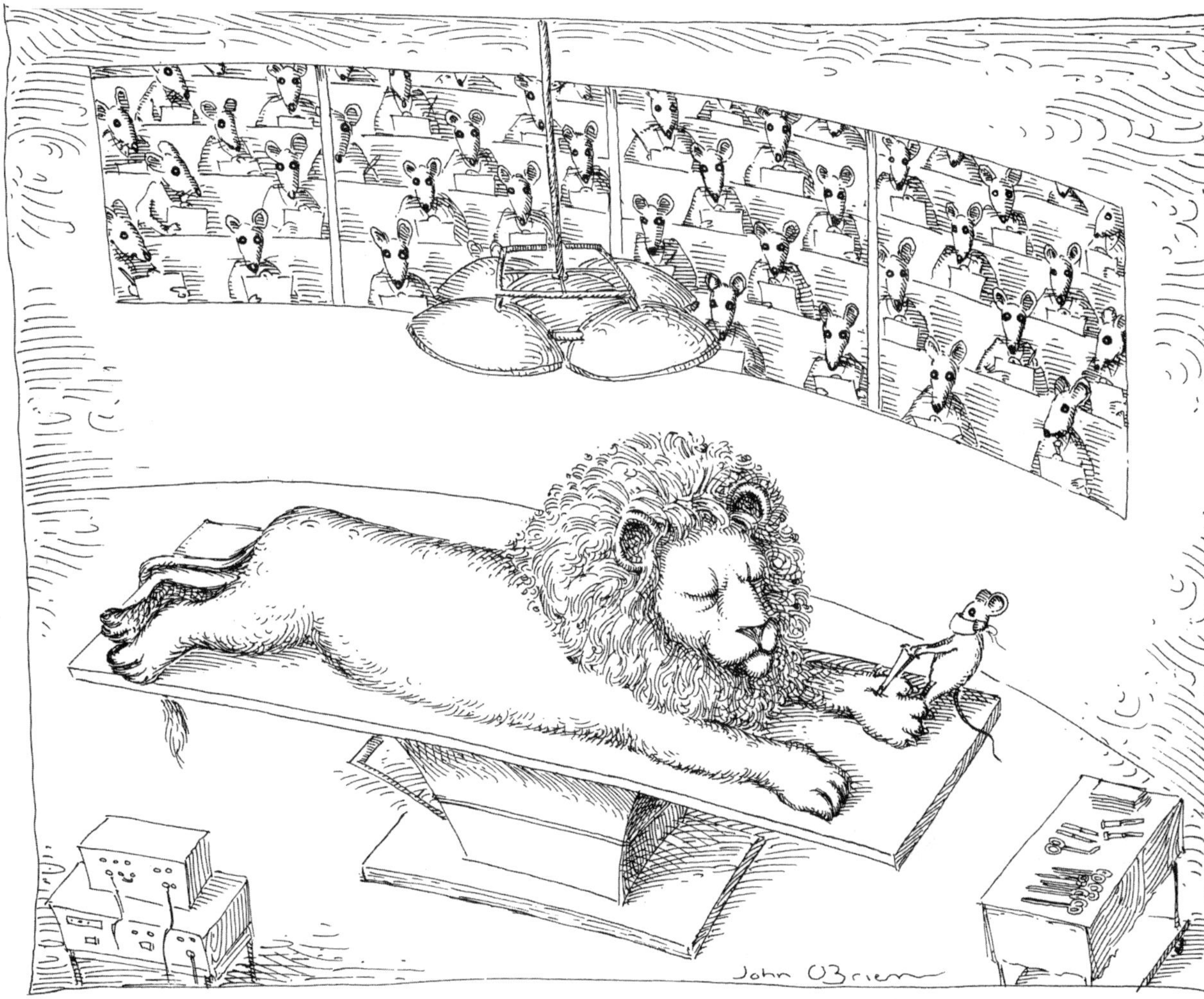
John O'Brien

"Hm-m-dum-di-dum-dum-dum—"

The stock-in-trade joke

MEDICAL MANNERS

Two billion little bugs

*The simple analogy of the Human Body
and the Motorcar*

The brisk arrival

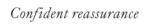

Confident reassurance

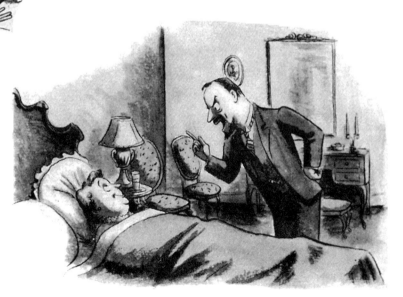

The good-natured scolding

"'I swear by Apollo Physician, by Asclepius, by Health, by Panacea, and by all the gods and goddesses, making them my witnesses, that I will carry out, according to my ability and judgment, this oath and this indenture. To hold my teacher in this art equal to my own parents; to make him partner in my livelihood; when he is in need of money to share mine with him; to consider his family as my own brothers, and to teach them this art, if they want to learn it, without fee or indenture. I will use treatment to help the sick according to my ability and judgment, but never with a view to injury and wrongdoing. I will keep pure and holy both my life and my art. In whatsoever houses I enter, I will enter to help the sick, and I will abstain from all intentional wrongdoing and harm. And whatsoever I shall see or hear in the course of my profession in my intercourse with men, if it be what should not be published abroad, I will never divulge, holding such things to be holy secrets. Now if I carry out this oath, and break it not, may I gain forever reputation among all men for my life and for my art; but if I transgress it and forswear myself, may the opposite befall me.' <u>Now</u> may I examine you?"

Dial 123-SICK and Reach Out to Your Fellow-Hypochondriacs

"*Frankly, Mr. Poole, I would strongly suggest you make one last, desperate bid for happiness.*"

"I hardly know how to say this, Mrs. Landecker, but what you've got
there is pre-patellar bursitis, or—er—a bad case of housemaid's knee."

47

"Dr. Gachet, call your office."

"I didn't say I ruled out the possibility of your having moon germs entirely. I merely said it was too early to tell whether you should be placed in quarantine."

*"But, J.G., if you told me once you told me a hundred times
you wanted adult Westerns."*

"There has been a sharp increase in his cantankerousness."

"I'm afraid a house call is out of the question just now, Comrade Koo. Try pushing the needle in a bit farther, wiggling it as you do so, and if the pain persists call me in the morning."

"In a case of this kind, Mrs. Hall, our first concern is to persuade the patient that he's a stala<u>gmite</u>."

"...and then I add the flour and shortening, and a tiny pinch of salt, of course.
Some people believe in baking it for at least an hour in a very hot oven, but..."

"I'd like you to have a CAT scan."

"Dr. Gorman? My name is Milton Kruger*, and I've been very troubled lately by an asterisk."

"Too much pasta. Go have some spare ribs."

"I think my fees will seem less unreasonable to you if you will stop to consider the many long and costly years a doctor must spend to prepare himself, and the tremendous day-by-day expenses a doctor has to face . . ."

"You don't know how lucky you are! A quarter of an inch either way, and it would have been outside the area of reimbursable coverage!"

"You'd love my Dr. Brodie. His creed is rest, rest, rest, and more rest."

"The ringing in your ears—I think I can help."

"I'd like you to see a botanist. You exhibit many of the symptoms of Dutch elm disease."

"*Doctor, have you any advice to offer a young man who would love to be a physician but whose crowded schedule simply doesn't permit time for medical school?*"

"Give it to me straight, Doc. How many more golden years
would you say I have staring me in the face?"

"It's just a question of directing that energy into another field—
quilting, for example."

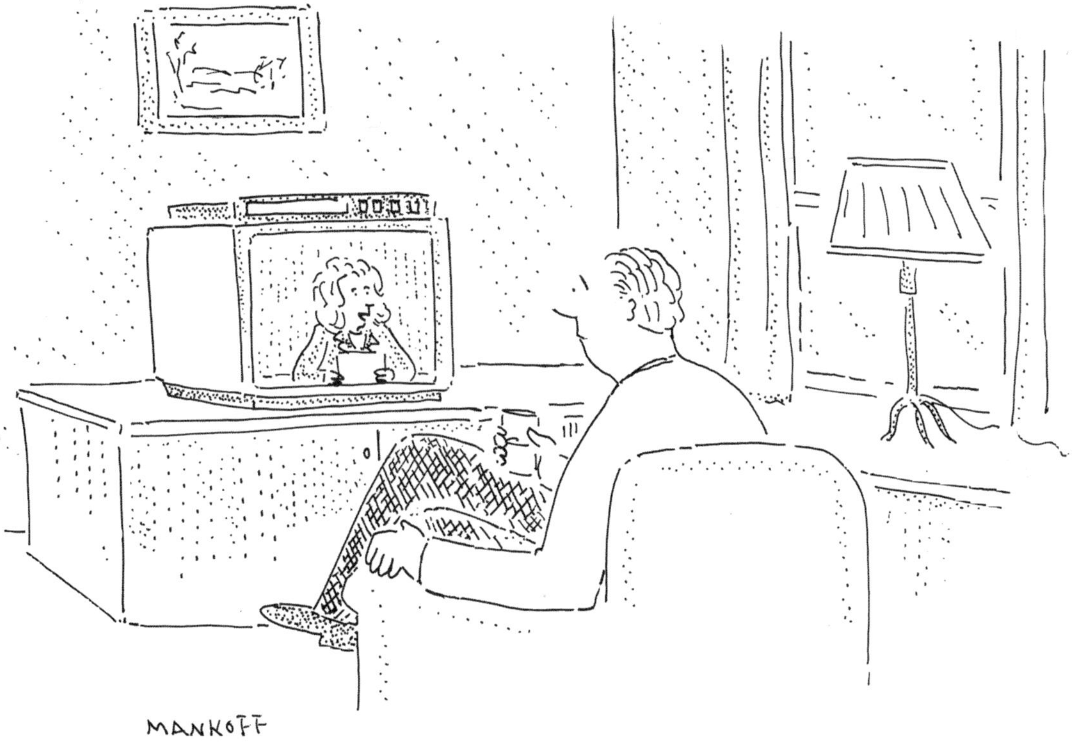
MANKOFF

"Doctors said that although the approach is still experimental, it may prove an effective weapon in the fight against heath-care reform."

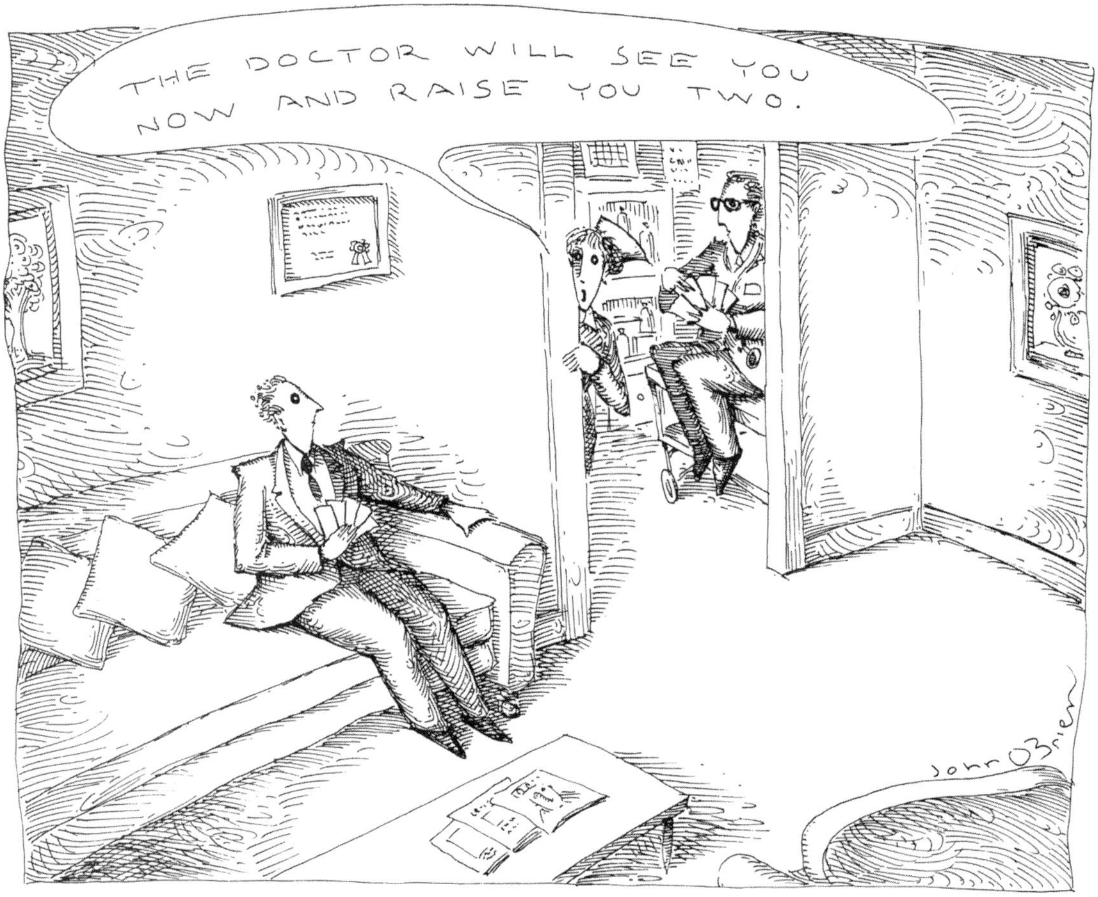
THE DOCTOR WILL SEE YOU NOW AND RAISE YOU TWO.
John O'Brien

"We doctors have our problems, too. For example, I have to be true not
only to the Hippocratic oath but to the A.M.A. as well."

"Now have this prescription filled and take as directed. Then two nights
after the first full moon, procure the left hind leg of a he-frog and a
root of St. John's-wort . . ."

"Tell you what I'm going to do. I'm going to pull you through."

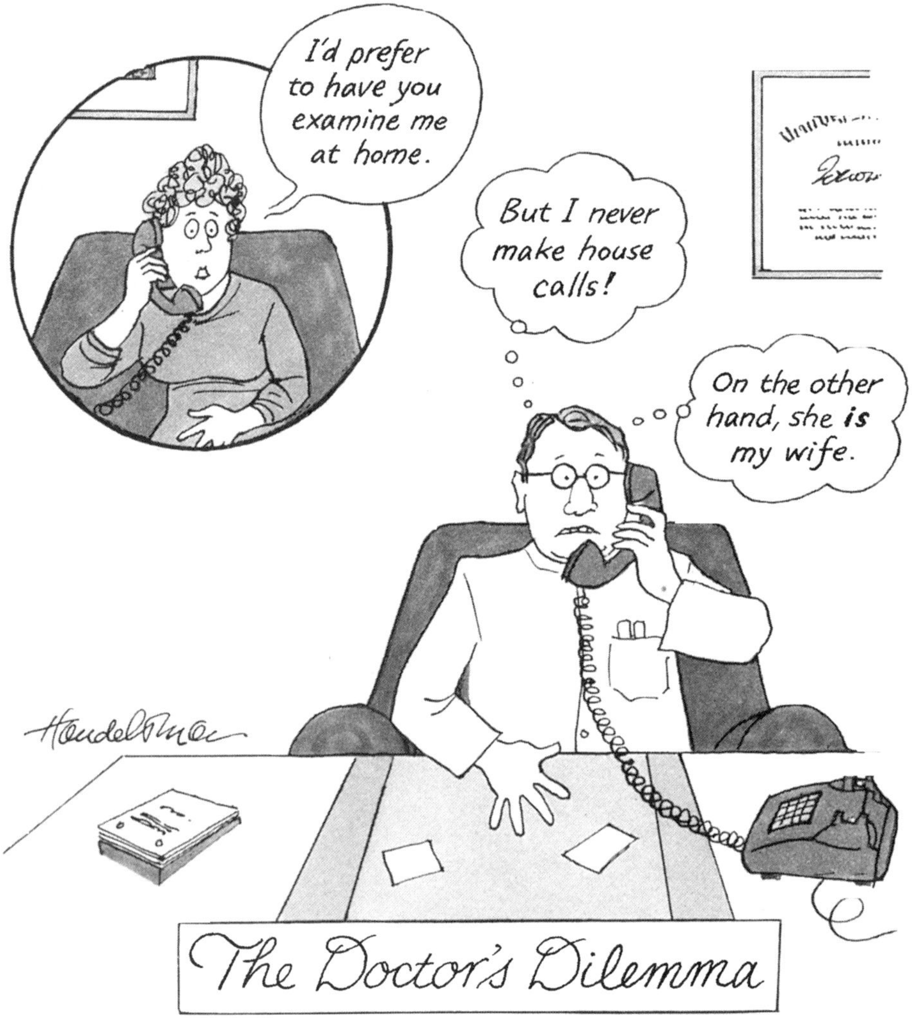
I'd prefer to have you examine me at home.
But I never make house calls!
On the other hand, she **is** my wife.
The Doctor's Dilemma

"When you say that I'm sound as a dollar, Doctor, just what do you mean?"

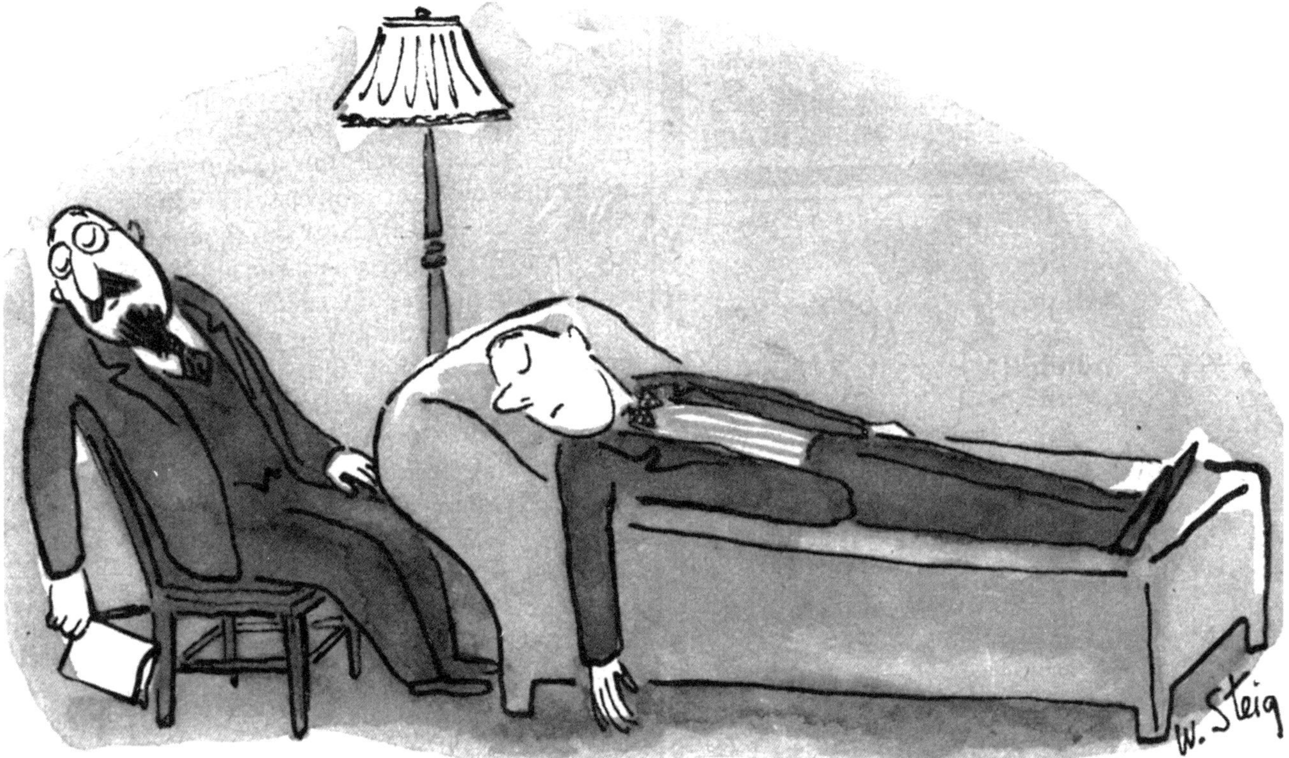
W. Steig

"Mind you, only <u>one</u> doctor out of ten recommends it."

"By all means, dear—buy it if you really want it. We'll find the money for it somehow."

"Has it ever occurred to you just to say, 'Hey, I quit. I don't want to be part of the food chain anymore'?"

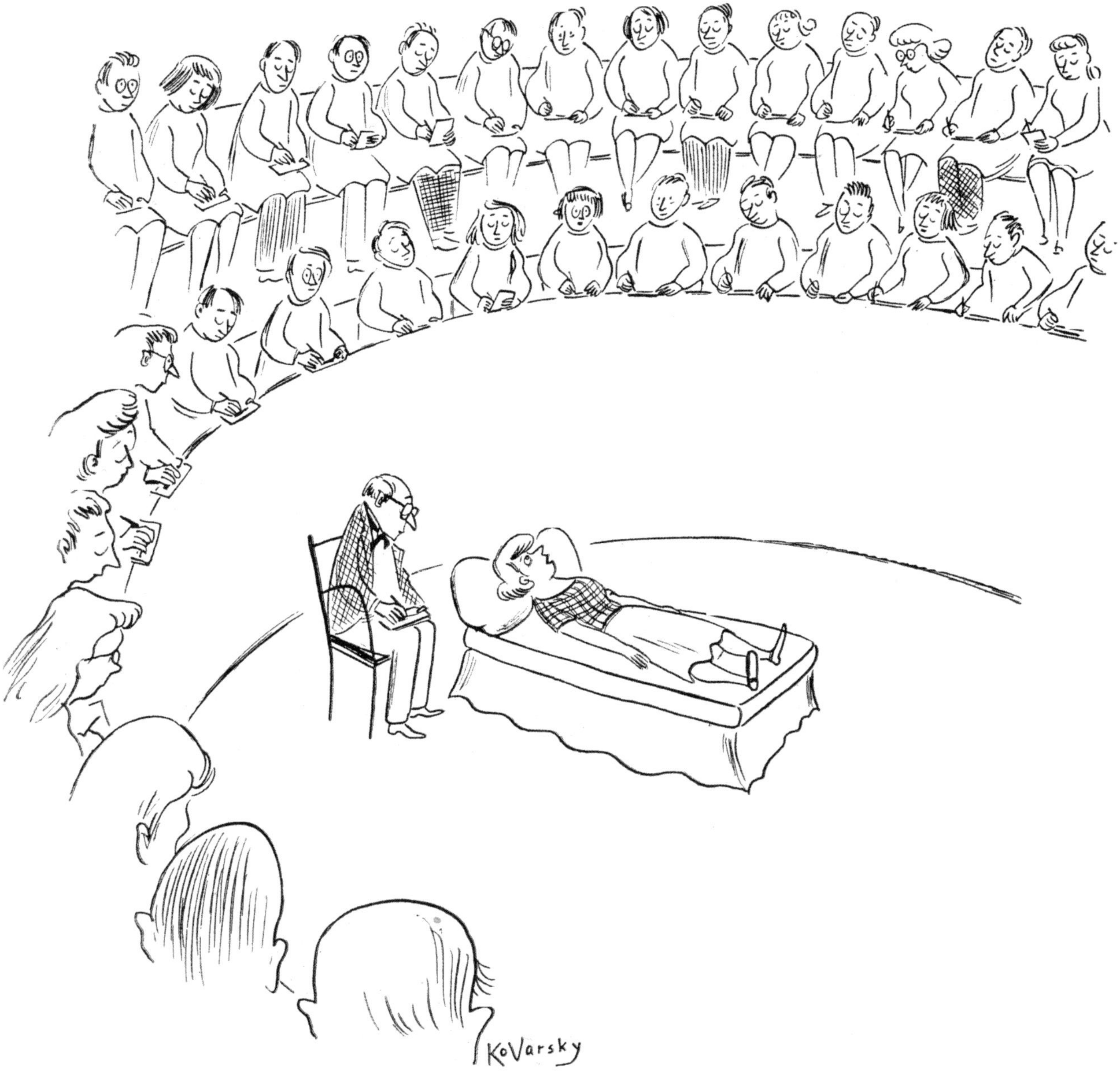
KoVarsky

"*You're not my patient, you're my meat, Mrs. Quist!*"

"You must try not to worry. Dr. Perry is doing everything humanly possible."

"I see by your copy of 'Newsweek' that Lyndon Johnson has decided
not to run for reëlection."

"Why do you think you cross the road?"

"I'm sorry. The doctor no longer makes phone calls."

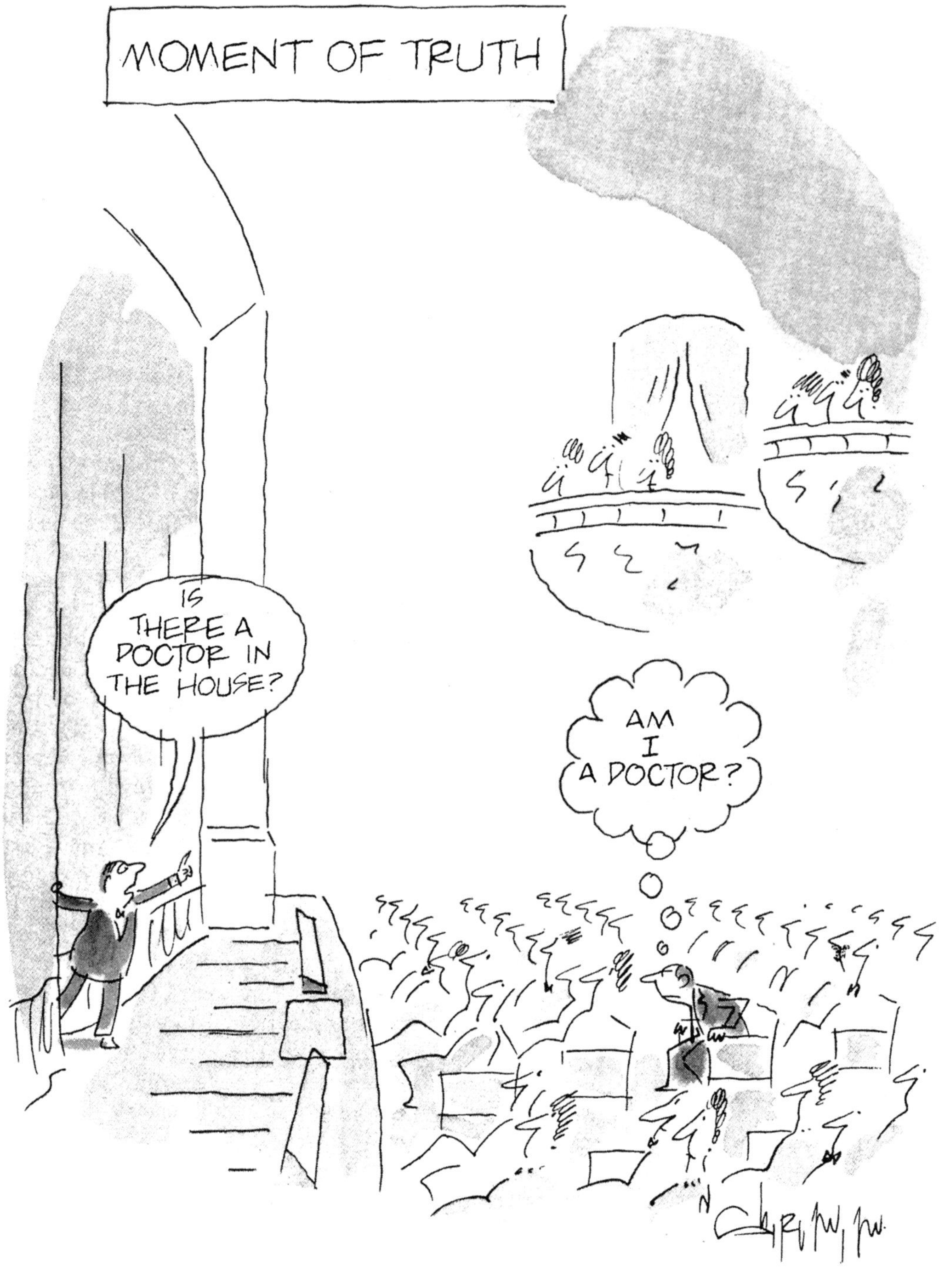
MOMENT OF TRUTH
IS THERE A DOCTOR IN THE HOUSE?
AM I A DOCTOR?

"You both appear to be in excellent health."

"Let me through! I'm a quack."

Index of Artists

The text of this book was set in a postscript version of Caslon Old Face No. 2
on a Macintosh. Printed and bound by Arcata Graphics/Martinsburg,
Martinsburg, West Virginia
Designed by Virginia Tan